AMENDMENTS TO THE UNITED STATES CONSTITUTION
THE BILL OF RIGHTS

THE RIGHT TO PRIVACY IN THE HOME

THE THIRD AMENDMENT

JASON PORTERFIELD

rosen publishing's
rosen
central

New York

Published in 2011 by The Rosen Publishing Group, Inc.
29 East 21st Street, New York, NY 10010

Library of Congress Cataloging-in-Publication Data

Porterfield, Jason.
The Third Amendment : the right to privacy in the home / Jason Porterfield. — 1st ed.
    p. cm. — (Amendments to the United States Constitution : the Bill of Rights)
Includes bibliographical references and index.
ISBN 978-1-4488-1256-1 (library binding)
ISBN 978-1-4488-2304-8 (pbk.)
ISBN 978-1-4488-2321-5 (6-pack)
1. United States. Constitution. 3rd Amendment—Juvenile literature. 2. Soldiers—Billeting—United States—Juvenile literature. 3. Privacy, Right of—United States—Juvenile literature. I. Title.
KF45583rd .P67 2011
342.7308'58—dc22

                                                                        2010015855

Manufactured in the United States of America

CPSIA Compliance Information: Batch #W11YA: For further information, contact Rosen Publishing, New York, New York, at 1-800-237-9932.

On the cover: A Shreveport, Louisiana, police officer looks through the window of a suspected drug house. Inset: Members of the Fundamentalist Church of Jesus Christ of Latter-Day Saints are rounded onto a bus after being held for allegations of abuse within the polygamous sect.

CONTENTS

4   INTRODUCTION

7   **CHAPTER ONE**
THE QUARTERING ACTS
AND THE AMERICAN
REVOLUTION

20   **CHAPTER TWO**
CRAFTING THE THIRD
AMENDMENT

33   **CHAPTER THREE**
THE EFFECTS OF THE
THIRD AMENDMENT

44   **CHAPTER FOUR**
THE THIRD AMENDMENT
TODAY

52   AMENDMENTS TO THE
U.S. CONSTITUTION

55   GLOSSARY

57   FOR MORE INFORMATION

60   FOR FURTHER READING

61   BIBLIOGRAPHY

63   INDEX

INTRODUCTION

I magine a nation in which soldiers could come to a person's home and demand shelter. The soldiers could settle in, eat the home-owner's food, and require that the homeowner provide any supplies necessary for the soldiers' comfort. In such a nation, the home-owner would have little choice but to obey the soldiers' demands. Homeowners would not be secure in their own homes and could become vulnerable to looting or acts of vandalism on the part of soldiers. Those who resisted could be punished by the military.

The Americans who lived through the days leading up to the Revolutionary War (1775–1783) endured such experiences under the British colonial government. They wanted to make sure that future

Members of the U.S. Air Force take part in a ceremony at Fairfield Air Force Base in Washington. The Third Amendment led the military to establish bases throughout the country.

generations would not have to as well. When writing the Bill of Rights, an amendment was included that gives citizens the right to refuse to shelter soldiers in their homes. The Third Amendment states that "no soldier shall, in time of peace, be quartered in any house, without the consent of the owner; nor in time of war, but in a manner to be prescribed by law." Quartering is allowed only during wartime, and even then only according to the law.

Today, few people are familiar with the Third Amendment. It seldom comes up in court cases and has received little media attention over the years. There have been few instances since the nineteenth century in which quartering for troops has been an issue, and the protections directly offered by the Third Amendment may appear to have little relevance to modern life. After all, modern military bases provide ample housing to personnel who need a place to stay. However, the amendment has helped guarantee this arrangement by restricting the military's ability to demand quarters from private citizens. The amendment continues to protect the rights of citizens and ensure that they remain safe in their own homes. The amendment allows military personnel to live as tenants in homes owned by others, so long as they have the permission of the homeowner. Along with several other amendments, it also protects citizens' right to privacy.

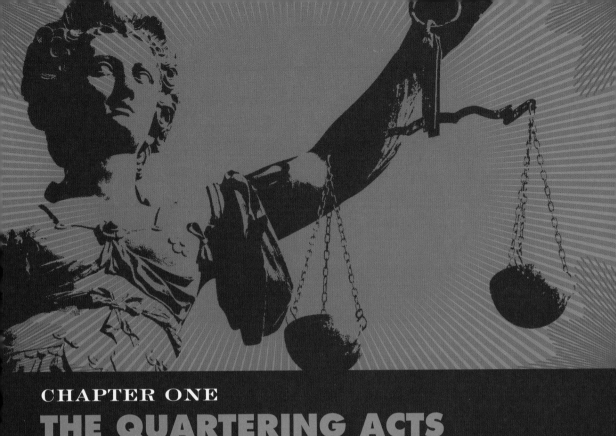

CHAPTER ONE

THE QUARTERING ACTS AND THE AMERICAN REVOLUTION

The American colonies were governed by England for more than 150 years with few objections from the colonists. Though the colonists lived thousands of miles away from England, they were happy to consider themselves English. This began changing in the 1760s, when the British government started taking a greater interest in controlling the colonies.

Life in Colonial America

By the mid-eighteenth century, relations between the American colonists and their rulers in Great Britain had become strained. The colonists saw themselves as key to the expansion of the British Empire. Away from the eastern coastal areas, North America was largely unexplored and sparsely settled by European colonists. The colonists viewed the Native Americans who had lived on the continent for thousands of years with fear and suspicion. The vast land west of the Appalachian Mountains was virtually unknown to the settlers.

Many colonists felt that the British Parliament and the royal family were out of touch with life in the colonies. Though separated from Great Britain by the vast Atlantic Ocean, most decisions about how the colonies were governed were made in London. Still, most colonists thought of themselves as English citizens. They believed in their right to participate in their own government.

The colonists had some measure of self-government. Colonial charters gave the thirteen colonies the right to maintain their own government assemblies, though decisions by these assemblies were understood to remain under control of the British Parliament. The colonial assemblies had authority only over their own affairs, and any legislation passed by an assembly had to be approved in England by the country's Board of Trade before it could go into effect. The

British Prime Minister William Pitt the Younger speaks to Parliament in this illustration from 1793. Prior to the American Revolution, many colonists resented their lack of representation in the British Parliament.

colonies were seen as a business venture, and the Board of Trade denied them the right to oversee matters relating to trade.

The assemblies operated much the same way as Parliament. Only free men who owned property had the right to vote or hold office. Women,

slaves, and indentured servants could not vote. However, the sheer size of the colonies allowed a much larger number of colonists to be property owners than in England, giving a larger portion of the population a voice in the political process.

Another factor that contributed to the growing sense of independence held by the colonists was the English government's neglect of the colonies. The colonies were mostly undeveloped and, compared to England, insignificant in terms of their population and economy. Beginning in the mid-1600s, the English government became preoccupied with its own affairs. These included the English Civil War (1641–1651) and a series of wars against France that were fought both in Europe and in the colonies with the help of the colonists. In the midst of this turmoil, the colonies were largely given free reign to oversee their affairs. Colonial governments made laws, regulated their own courts and militias, established new counties, and raised revenue to pay the costs of government with little oversight from England.

This pattern continued for about 120 years, until the end of the French and Indian War (1754–1763), which forced France to give up its claim to land east of the Mississippi River.

The British fought for control of the North American colonies during the French and Indian War. Colonists and their Native American allies fought alongside British soldiers against the French.

The war was very expensive for the British, who wanted the colonists to help pay the expense in return for preventing a French takeover of the colonies. At this time, the British also realized the growing importance of raw materials, such as timber and iron ore, which were imported

from America. Great Britain began moving to tighten its hold on the colonies.

The colonists, however, resisted these efforts. They felt that they had already contributed to the war effort by providing supplies and troops for the colonial militias, which fought beside British troops. They also did not believe that they had profited from the outcome of the war.

Unrest in the Colonies

Soon after the war ended, the British government began imposing new restrictions on the colonists. Parliament's Proclamation Act of 1763 forbade colonists from settling west of the Appalachian Mountains. The act angered colonists, who believed they had risked their lives to drive the French from the region. Another law, the Sugar Act of 1764, enforced the collection of a tax on molasses brought into the colonies from the Caribbean. The colonists felt that the tax was imposed unjustly without their consent.

Anger in the colonies continued to grow as Great Britain exercised its right to impose taxes and regulations on the colonists. In 1765, Parliament passed the Stamp Act and the Mutiny Act. The Stamp Act required that all documents, such as newspapers, wills, and court orders, carry a special stamp. The stamps could only be bought with silver coins, rather than with the paper money and barter system that many colonists used.

The colonists were furious about the Stamp Act, though a similar act had been in place in England for centuries and the stamps sold in the colonies were cheaper than those sold in England. Colonists referred to the Stamp Act and the earlier taxes as "taxation without representation." They felt it was unfair that they should be taxed by Parliament without having a member of Parliament representing their interests. Colonists protested loudly about the act, sometimes forming angry mobs and attacking tax collectors.

The British government had not anticipated such a reaction and moved to lift the tax in 1766. However, other taxes and laws passed during the 1760s remained in place and continued to anger colonists.

The Mutiny Act

Of the acts that remained in place, none had a greater impact than the Quartering Act, also known as the Mutiny Act. The Quartering Act required that the colonial assemblies set aside money to house the British troops stationed in the colonies and provide them with food and supplies. Ordinarily, British soldiers in the colonies were housed in buildings called barracks, where dozens of soldiers could live at one time. However, if there were more soldiers stationed in a town than there were barracks, they were to be moved into such buildings as inns, barns, and empty houses.

The law was passed by Parliament as a means to ensure that the colonies paid for their own military protection. Colonial leaders, however, argued that they provided their own defense through militias made up of armed colonists. They resented having to pay to house soldiers whom they felt were not needed. They also felt that the act violated English laws dating back to 1111, when the London city charter forbade the quartering of soldiers within the city walls. The English Bill of Rights of 1689 also made quartering illegal, though the law's reach was never extended to any of the British colonies.

Colonists also interpreted the Quartering Act as a way to control them by presenting a show of force. At the time, the British government

British soldiers march through New York City in 1776. The British already had a large military force in the colonies when the Revolutionary War began.

kept a standing army of ten thousand soldiers in the colonies. Other laws passed around the same time gave the British greater power to conduct trials without juries and to limit the freedom of the press. Protests continued throughout the colonies, and anti-British sentiment grew.

Citizens and Soldiers in Conflict

In 1768, the Massachusetts House of Representatives sent a petition to King George III asking for the repeal of the laws and sent a letter to the other colonies asking them to join in the resistance. The British responded in May 1768 by sending the warship HMS *Romney* to Boston Harbor to protect the customs officials who were responsible for collecting taxes for the government. On June 10, the *Romney* seized a ship belonging to Boston merchant John Hancock called the *Liberty* on suspicion that it was being used to smuggle goods into the colony without paying the necessary taxes and duties. Angry citizens began rioting, and customs officials were forced to retreat to nearby Castle William for protection.

In response to the riots, General Thomas Gage, the British commander in chief over North America, was instructed to use whatever force he felt necessary to bring the colony back under control. That October, the first of four British army regiments arrived in Boston to keep the peace. Two of the regiments were removed the following year, but the others remained behind.

Tensions between the colonists and the soldiers stationed in Boston finally boiled over on March 5, 1770. An angry mob formed at the city's Custom House after a guard attacked a group of boys who had been taunting him. The mob grew to an estimated three hundred to four hundred people. The soldiers who responded to the incident eventually opened fire on the crowd, hitting eleven men. Three were killed at the scene, and another two later died of their wounds. This incident would become known as the Boston Massacre.

The Boston Massacre was used as a rallying point by colonial figures such as Samuel Adams and Paul Revere to fuel rebellious sentiment. All

but two of the soldiers accused of firing the shots were tried and acquitted. Colonists who had been indifferent to the British presence saw the violent incident as an unnecessary show of force in the city's streets. If the Quartering Act had not been passed, the British soldiers would have been garrisoned outside of the city.

Later incidents of colonial unrest in Massachusetts would lead the British to pass stronger laws. The most famous of these events is the Boston Tea Party. In 1773, Parliament's passage of the Tea Act made the East India Company the only company that could sell tea in the colonies. The colonists would pay less for their tea, though the price would include a small duty, or tax. The colonists protested strongly against the tax. In New York City and Philadelphia, they refused to unload the ships carrying the tea. In Boston, colonists famously boarded tea ships at night and threw the tea into the harbor.

The British government came down on the colonists by passing a set of laws called the Coercive Acts, which were designed to strengthen the authority of British officials. The laws focused on Boston, which was the center of much of the colonial unrest. The acts closed the Port of Boston and rewrote Massachusetts's colonial

Colonists increased their opposition to the presence of British soldiers after the Boston Massacre, seen here in this illustration from 1770. The British responded by introducing harsher laws in the colonies, including the Quartering Act of 1774.

charter, strengthening the authority of royal officials at the expense of the colony's elected assembly. The acts also allowed royal officials who committed a crime in Massachusetts to be tried in England, rather than in the colony.

More restrictive laws followed. A law called the Quebec Act, passed in 1774, stated that the territory between the Ohio and Mississippi rivers acquired during the French and Indian War would be overseen by British officials in Canada, rather than in the thirteen lower colonies. Any settlers who moved into the territory would lose the right to elected representation.

The Quartering Act of 1774

The British passed a second quartering act aimed at quieting the protests in Massachusetts. The Quartering Act of 1774 expanded the earlier Quartering Act. Like the first law, it stated that soldiers who demanded shelter be provided with suitable quarters within twenty-four hours. If suitable barracks were not provided for soldiers, the soldiers were to be put up in empty houses, outbuildings, and inns. The act went further than the previous law. It stated that the owners of the properties were directly responsible for making sure that the soldiers were fed and supplied with clothing, equipment, and other necessities.

Along with the other laws, the Quartering Act was labeled one of the "Intolerable Acts" by the colonists. In 1774, delegates from each of the colonies except Georgia met in Philadelphia to discuss a response to the laws. Acting together, the delegates to this First Continental Congress decided to boycott British imports and send a list of resolutions called the Declaration of Rights and Grievances to Great Britain. Parliament rejected the declaration, and on April 19, 1775, the Revolutionary War broke out between the British and the colonists in Massachusetts at the Battles of Lexington and Concord.

The Articles of Confederation

The Articles of Confederation were intended to legitimize the Continental Congress's powers to raise military forces, establish trade regulations, send out ambassadors, and issue money. They also changed the designation of the colonies to states. They were supposed to draw the states together in a common cause.

The articles had originally called for a strong central government but ultimately created a loose association—or confederation—of individual political units. The individual states maintained their own sovereignty and were essentially independent nations, while the central government remained very weak. Congress could not collect taxes from the state or enforce any laws it passed and could not make any treaties that restricted the ability of states to control trade. States had the right to recall their representatives at any time and even had the power to withdraw from the rest of the country. States even began passing laws against one another as resentments grew. Congress recognized that a stronger form of government was needed to unite the states.

The delegates met again that May as the Second Continental Congress and decided to take steps toward independence. They raised an army, established trade regulations, sent ambassadors to other nations, and encouraged the colonies to set up local governments. In 1776, the delegates ratified the Declaration of Independence, a document that set forth the reasons for breaking free from Great Britain, including their objection to quartering troops. The delegates also began working on a document called the Articles of Confederation and Perpetual Union that would serve as a forerunner to the U.S. Constitution. Ratified in 1781, the articles formally created the United States of America.

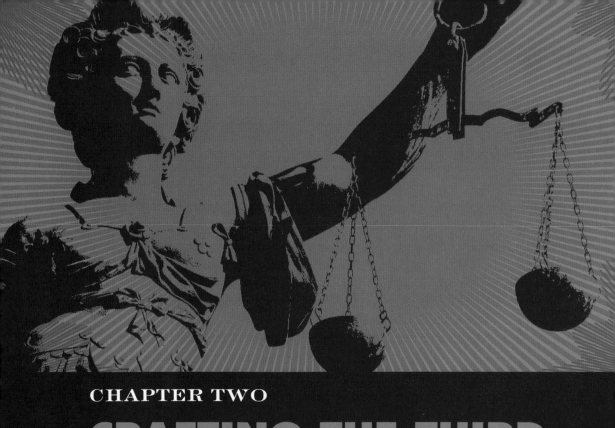

CHAPTER TWO

CRAFTING THE THIRD AMENDMENT

W hile the Articles of Confederation established the federal government and held the colonies together in a loose union, the document complicated many government functions. Problems often arose among the new states as they sought control of western lands and passed laws against each other.

In 1787, delegates from twelve states (Rhode Island was not represented) met in Philadelphia for a national conference established by the Continental Congress. The delegates were given the task of strengthening and improving the Articles of Confederation. In all, fifty-five delegates attended the convention, including leaders such as George Washington, Thomas Jefferson, and Benjamin Franklin.

The Constitutional Convention

The Constitutional Convention met from May 25 to September 17, 1787. While the original purpose of the convention was simply to consider amending the Articles of Confederation, it ultimately resulted in radical changes to the government. The delegates themselves represented a broad range of opinions about the nation's future. They wanted what they believed to be the best outcome for their states on matters such as representation in Congress. Debate went on for days—and sometimes weeks—on matters such as whether or not to forbid slavery.

One of the most influential delegates was James Madison of Virginia. Madison had studied governments around the world and believed that the United States needed a strong central government. He wrote a series of fifteen resolutions called the Virginia Plan that proposed drastic changes to the government. The Virginia Plan proposed that the federal government have the power to make laws and enforce them through the executive and judicial branches. It also proposed the establishment of a bicameral Congress. While the states would retain many of their powers, they would also be part of a national government. Madison's Virginia Plan would ultimately form the basis of the federal government.

The document was finally completed and signed on September 17, 1787. However, the work of the delegates had not ended. They had to return to their states and have the new document ratified, or approved, before it could become law. When nine of the thirteen states ratified the document, the Constitution would be considered accepted and a new government would be formed.

However, the delegates had their work cut out for them. The colonial conventions disagreed about the proposed national government. One faction, called the Federalists, believed in the concept of a strong central government. The Anti-Federalists wanted the states to

Federalist James Madison is widely known as the Father of the Constitution and as the author of the Bill of Rights. He was elected president of the United States in 1808.

remain in control of their own destiny while staying loosely united. The Federalists ultimately won the debate by presenting a formal plan of government, gaining the support of land-owning men who could vote, and through the persuasive arguments of famous Federalists such as Benjamin Franklin, Alexander Hamilton, James Madison, and George Washington.

By July 1788, all of the states had ratified the Constitution except North Carolina and Rhode Island. These two states waited until after the inauguration of George Washington as the first president of the United States in 1789. However, even after the U.S. Constitution had been ratified by all thirteen states, some leaders continued to criticize the document for not doing enough to protect individual freedoms.

The Federalist Papers

During the process of ratifying the Constitution, Alexander Hamilton and other Federalists worried that the document would be rejected because it called for a strong central government. Hamilton felt that he needed to create strong public support for the document to guarantee its ratification. Hamilton, James Madison, and John Jay wrote a series of eighty-five articles that attempted to explain the strengths of the Constitution and why the document was needed. The essays were printed in several newspapers between October 1787 and August 1788. The authors wished to keep their identities secret and published the essays under the pseudonym Publicus.

The essays were used in the debate over ratification in New York and Virginia. Today, they are considered among the most important writings about the Constitution and are still used by the Supreme Court to determine the intentions of the Founding Fathers. The fact that the essays argued against passage of a Bill of Rights shows that a lively debate continued over the need for such a document.

The Bill of Rights

Some of the Founding Fathers decided that they needed to win over the most prominent critics of the Constitution, otherwise the young nation ran the risk of breaking apart. These critics (among them Thomas Jefferson) thought that the Constitution should guarantee specific rights. They wanted a Bill of Rights to protect citizens and ensure that the nation's government would never become tyrannical, as they felt Great Britain's had in the years leading up to the Revolutionary War.

However, others objected to the idea of a Bill of Rights. They worried that, by attaching a list of rights to the Constitution, they would limit protection only to those rights. However, similar bills had already been passed. In fact, the colonists had lived under such a bill until the Revolutionary War. In 1689, Parliament passed the English Bill of Rights to protect the basic freedoms of English subjects.

As the thirteen colonies began breaking away from Great Britain in 1776, George Mason referred to the English Bill of Rights when drafting the Virginia Bill of Rights. The Virginia Bill of Rights outlined the right to life, liberty, and property and described government as being the servant of the people. Mason's document influenced Thomas Jefferson as he wrote the Declaration of Independence and influenced the creation of the Bill of Rights. Mason was among the delegates to the Constitutional Convention who did not sign the document because it did not include a bill of rights.

James Madison took up the work of creating the Bill of Rights. He began by taking suggestions from other Founding Fathers who felt that individual freedoms needed to be protected. Madison condensed these suggestions and presented them to Congress as a Bill of Rights amending the Constitution on June 8, 1789. Congress approved twelve of the amendments and sent them out to the states to be ratified. All thirteen

In 1776, Thomas Jefferson wrote the Declaration of Independence, which influenced James Madison's work on the Bill of Rights. Jefferson and other Anti-Federalists opposed ratifying the Constitution without including a bill of rights.

states ratified ten of the amendments, and they went into effect in 1791 as the Bill of Rights.

Protecting Basic Freedoms

The Bill of Rights is one of the most famous documents in the nation's history. Many of the amendments in the bill were written as a direct response to the pre–Revolutionary War laws passed by the British. The Founding Fathers wanted to guarantee that citizens would not have to live through a similar loss of liberties. Amendments that specifically protected basic freedoms included the First Amendment, which guarantees freedom of speech, press, religion, assembly, and petition; the Second Amendment, which guarantees the right to bear arms; and the Fourth Amendment, which prohibits unreasonable searches and seizures of property. The Bill of Rights states that people have rights not specifically listed and that the federal government derives its power solely from the Constitution.

A Response to the Quartering Acts

Like the Fourth Amendment, the Third Amendment was drafted as a direct response to the Quartering Acts. These acts proved to be a major burden to colonists before the Revolutionary War.

The presence of the soldiers in towns and on private property was supposed to make the colonists less likely to rise up against the government. British officials reasoned that by quartering soldiers with known troublemakers, they could possibly put an end to the civil unrest that was threatening their control of the colonies. They also believed that since the British army had fought to defend the colonies from the French

NOTHING WAS THOUGHT OF BUT THIS TAXATION,
AND THE EASIEST METHOD OF LIQUIDATION.

T-A-X

'TWAS ENOUGH TO VEX
THE SOULS OF THE MEN OF BOSTON TOWN,
TO READ THIS UNDER THE SEAL OF THE CROWN.

TAX·ON·
TEA·
3ᵈ per lb

1773

THEY WERE LOYAL SUBJECTS OF GEORGE THE THIRD;
SO THEY BELIEVED AND SO THEY AVERRED,
BUT THIS BRISTLING, OFFENSIVE PLACARD SET
ON THE WALLS, WAS WORSE THAN A BAYONET,

The colonists were unhappy with the new taxes imposed on them. The British believed that quartering soldiers in towns and cities would keep the colonists from rebelling. However, the soldiers became targets for angry colonists.

during the French and Indian War, the colonists should provide some portion of the army's upkeep while troops were stationed there.

Many colonists had remained deeply loyal to the British government, and many colonial leaders wanted to make peace with the British. However, the British had greatly miscalculated the colonists' feelings about British soldiers living in their midst. This was particularly true in the Massachusetts colony and in the city of Boston, where anti-British sentiment ran high.

During the Revolutionary War, both British and American soldiers were quartered with private citizens. Soldiers from George Washington's Continental Army were quartered in private homes by the New York Provincial Congress. However, Washington and other American military leaders opposed the practice of quartering. They largely avoided the situation by staying away from towns, using public buildings, and building their own barracks. As a result, American troops were seldom quartered with private citizens. The relatively few instances of quartering occurred early in the war, before the states had a chance to make provisions for housing soldiers.

By the time the war ended, the governments of Delaware, Massachusetts, and Maryland had passed laws to protect citizens from having to quarter troops during peacetime. The laws did allow for quartering troops in times of war, but only under the direction of the state legislatures.

Introducing the Third Amendment

James Madison himself introduced the Third Amendment after repeatedly hearing concerns that soldiers could be quartered in private homes. The British Quartering Act was still very fresh in the minds of citizens and lawmakers, though the U.S. Army consisted largely of local militias at the time.

The Third Amendment met with little resistance from leaders who did not want their fragile new nation to be threatened by worries that they were about to repeat the same mistakes that the British had made. However, the amendment specifically prohibited quartering during times of peace, leaving open the possibility that soldiers could be quartered in private homes during times of war. Madison and other leaders recognized that their new nation faced threats on its northern border, where Great Britain still held Canada, and to the west, where France owned the territory west of the Mississippi River. Spain also held territories nearby.

Despite threats from European powers holding bordering territories and from hostile Native American tribes on the western frontier, some leaders objected to the idea of having a standing army at all. They argued that the army would lead the fledgling government to abuse its power over its citizens and that it would not be long before these soldiers would be quartered in towns and on private property.

Those that opposed maintaining a standing army instead wanted to use a militia system for defense. Militias would take part in occasional training exercises but would only actively serve when called to duty in times of war. In times of peace, they would go about their daily lives as private citizens. Because they would remain private citizens most of the time, militia men had to provide their own food, shelter, and supplies, freeing the government from the responsibility of doing so and from the possibility of ever passing a law similar to the Quartering Act.

Other leaders felt that it was absolutely necessary to maintain a regular, well-trained standing army. They knew that the threat from other nations was too great to rely on private citizens who may or may not be able to perform their militia duties if needed. Though he publicly praised militias, George Washington himself wrote privately to other leaders and urged them to support maintaining a standing army.

Alternate Versions

Three versions of the Third Amendment were proposed. Each forbade quartering without consent during peacetime. However, they differed on quartering during times of war. Madison himself proposed the first version in a speech to the House of Representatives. This version stated that "no soldiers shall in time of peace be quartered in any house without the consent of the owner; nor at any time, but in a manner warranted by law."

The vagueness of Madison's original version left it open to broad interpretation. Madison wanted to clarify gray areas in the amendment, such as whether or not troops could be quartered in homes during times of civil unrest when the rights of property owners may be threatened, such as during riots.

A second version, forwarded by representatives from Maryland and New Hampshire, clearly prohibited all quartering without consent during peacetime but said nothing about what to do during wartime. A third version of the amendment appeared in proposals from Virginia, New York, and North Carolina. It specified that troops could be quartered during wartime, but "only as the laws direct." This version was meant to place control of quartering during wartime in the hands of Congress should the need arise. This version was eventually combined with Madison's version to create the Third Amendment as it exists today.

Ultimately, it was decided that during times of peace, soldiers would be garrisoned in forts and camps close to towns and cities (and even within their borders), but that their quarters would be kept entirely

Many of the military bases in nineteenth-century America were walled fortresses located near ports and harbors. They were designed to protect shipping routes around important cities.

separate from private property. Soldiers could also seek lodgings on their own, but they would not be able to demand them as British soldiers had done and would have to pay their own expenses. The language of the amendment specifically states that soldiers cannot demand shelter from private citizens in peacetime.

The wording of the amendment leaves open the possibility of quartering during wartime. Madison and other Founding Fathers recognized that the young nation might have to fight again for its independence. While the British had left forts and garrison buildings throughout their former colonies, there could be no guarantee that any fighting that might occur would take place near such structures. In such cases, soldiers might have needed to use private homes or buildings for officer headquarters, storage, or even as hospitals.

CHAPTER THREE

THE EFFECTS OF THE THIRD AMENDMENT

The Third Amendment is one of the least ambiguous amendments in the Bill of Rights. Its intended purpose was to put to rest any fears that the strong federal government created by the Constitution would become tyrannical, as the Founding Fathers felt the British Parliament had become in its dealings with the colonies. The question of quartering troops during times of war has not been an issue since the Civil War (1861–1865) and has been directly addressed in only one Supreme Court case. Though seldom mentioned in the press or cited in court cases, the amendment remains vital by guaranteeing that the government takes care of its military personnel.

Housing Soldiers

The Third Amendment requires that, to stay in a home during peace-time, a soldier must have the consent of the property owner. Soldiers and other military personnel who rent or lease their quarters from a landlord are bound by the same legal obligations as other tenants. It is understood that they occupy their dwelling with the consent of their landlord, who maintains the right to evict them if just cause is found, as with any other tenant.

Many full-time military service members today live in quarters located on military bases, though some service members are allowed to

These new homes, located on Bolling Air Force Base in Washington, D.C., were constructed to replace older housing units. These homes give service members and their families a safe place to live.

live off base. These arrangements free the military from worrying about possible Third Amendment violations. Other military personnel may live rent-free with their family members, again provided they have the consent of the property owner or own their own homes.

For personnel in the National Guard or reserve forces who are not full-time members of the service, a clear distinction is made between when they are on active duty and when they are not. When on active duty, these service members are housed on military bases. At other times, they are left to make their own housing arrangements.

Amendment Use and Abuse

During a time of war, soldiers can be quartered in private homes, though such a case has not occurred since the nineteenth century. According to the Bill of Rights, when quartering is allowed, it is supposed to be regulated under rules set forth by Congress. During the War of 1812 (1812–1815), the United States had formally declared war against Great Britain. Congress failed to set forth any regulations for the act of quartering, but soldiers were quartered in private homes at the time.

Quartering was widespread during the Civil War, when hundreds of thousands of Union soldiers marched into the South to force the Confederacy to rejoin the United States. Both armies constantly took advantage of private property during the war. They camped and fought on farmers' fields, fed themselves on crops and livestock, and commandeered private houses and other buildings for their own use.

The Union Army faced unique circumstances during the Civil War. The federal government had not recognized the South's right to secede from the Union. This meant that the eleven states making up the Confederacy were still—in the eyes of Congress—part of the United

Union forces occupy a hillside in Confederate territory during the Civil War. Armies on both sides of the conflict occupied private homes, buildings, and land during the war.

States. However, the Confederacy now saw itself as an independent entity. The Confederate states had set up their own government, raised an army, and printed currency. They had control of forts and other federal facilities located in the South. They considered the Union Army to be an invading force. President Abraham Lincoln and Congress were faced with the unpleasant choice of either disregarding the Third Amendment—and a number of other constitutional rights—or allowing the South to break away. Northern soldiers were even quartered on private lands in states that had remained loyal to the Union.

In 1869, four years after the Civil War ended, the Supreme Court heard the case of *Texas v. White*. This case concerned the illegal sale of government-issued bonds during the Civil War by the state of Texas, which had seceded from the Union to join the Confederacy. The Court ruled that the act of seceding from the Union was not a right granted to states by the Constitution. Therefore, Texas had never legally left the Union and any actions taken by the state government at the time were void.

The court also ruled that by suspending its prewar government, Texas had dissolved the existing relationship between itself and the United States. The Constitution grants the United States the power to put down rebellions and guarantee that every state has a republican form of government. As a result, the U.S. government was obligated to take measures to restore the proper relationship with Texas. The ruling served to justify the federal government's suspension of the Bill of Rights in the rebel states.

However, the ruling did not extend to violations of the rights of citizens in states that had remained loyal. Quartering was widespread in the North, and the army seized the homes of loyal citizens to use as barracks. This practice was so common that the military even created a system for handling rent claims resulting from the seizure and use of homes by the military. Ultimately, about $500,000 in claims for rent and damage to property came in from property owners in Union states, and another $2.5 million came in from homeowners in Confederate states.

There was some question as to whether the quartering of soldiers on the property of loyal citizens was a violation of the Third Amendment. Technically, Congress never declared war on the Confederacy and saw the Civil War as an act of putting down an insurrection, rather than a full-on military conquest. Though the act of secession by the South created a state of war, Congress never acted to regulate quartering on Union territory. Instead, it was left to the executive branch—President Abraham Lincoln and his cabinet—to judge that the state of civil unrest was so great and the threat that it posed to the nation was serious enough to permit the act of quartering.

The Third Amendment and Civil Unrest

During the early days of the United States, acts of civil unrest were fairly common. People who had grievances against the government often took to the streets in protest. Such acts had helped spark the Revolutionary War. The Founding Fathers understood the importance of allowing citizens the right to protest, but they also recognized the danger presented by out-of-control mobs. They were aware of the threat posed by small separatist movements and small-scale conflicts with Native Americans. In such cases, the government responded with force and without consideration of Third Amendment rights.

The final version of the Third Amendment left out any mention of how the government should deal with domestic unrest, and no record exists of the Founding Fathers' intentions in these cases. They may have assumed that the executive branch would have the power to deal with quartering under such circumstances. Another possibility is that the language

During John Brown's attempted Harpers Ferry uprising in 1859, marines acted quickly to put down the insurrection and capture Brown's followers.

was intentionally left vague in order to guarantee that the amendment
would pass.

In 1807, Congress passed the Insurrection Act. This enabled the
president to deploy troops to put down a domestic insurrection. The law

limited the president's power by relying on local and state governments to provide the first response in such cases.

Posse Comitatus Act

The Posse Comitatus Act dealt with the question of quartering troops during an insurrection or other civil emergency. Passed in 1878, this law severely limited the federal government's ability to use the military for law enforcement purposes. The law forbids active members of the military and National Guard units under federal control from exercising the powers of law enforcement personnel while on nonfederal

The Third Amendment in Action: *Engblom v. Carey*

In 1982, the Second Circuit U.S. Court of Appeals heard the case of *Engblom v. Carey*. The case is the only lawsuit involving the quartering of soldiers to ever make it to a federal court of appeals. The case involved a 1979 strike by prison guards in New York. Governor Hugh Carey called in the National Guard to replace the guards who had left their jobs. The government ordered guards who lived at the prison in housing provided by the state to clear out of the houses to give the soldiers a place to stay.

Two of the guards sued the state, claiming that their Third Amendment rights had been violated because their homes had been occupied by soldiers against their wishes. The case was heard first by a district court, which threw it out because the guards did not own their homes at the prison. The appeals court ruled that the amendment applies to tenants, and, that under the amendment, National Guard personnel are considered soldiers. It sent the case back to the district court, where it was rejected on a legal technicality—that the guards failed to show that the state knew that it was violating their rights.

property, unless they are expressly authorized to do so by Congress or the Constitution.

The Posse Comitatus Act was pushed by members of Congress from the former Confederate states after the end of Reconstruction. The Reconstruction era was a period of time during which the Union army occupied the South to guarantee that slaves freed after the Civil War would be granted their rights as set forth by the Constitution. Many Southerners resented this presence and wanted to guarantee that the federal government would never again be able to occupy the Southern states as a police force.

The act effectively removed federal troops from many peacetime actions, largely putting the question of quartering troops to rest. The U.S. Air Force, Navy, and Marine Corps were later included in the act. In September 2005, President George W. Bush asked Congress to update federal laws to allow the military to restore and keep order in flood-ravaged New Orleans after Hurricane Katrina. The changes were made and passed in October 2006 but repealed in 2008.

The Third Amendment in Court

Today, the Third Amendment is among the least-cited amendments to the Constitution. Since the Civil War, there have been no widespread instances of quartering in private homes. Unlike other amendments, it has seldom come up before the Supreme Court. The handful of court decisions that have drawn on the amendment have mostly dealt with matters far removed from quartering troops.

In 1965, the Supreme Court ruled in the case of *Griswold v. Connecticut*. The Court's ruling found that a Connecticut law making it illegal for married couples to use birth control was unconstitutional

The *Eisenstadt v. Baird* case set a precedent for a number of landmark cases that continue to be controversial today, including the Supreme Court decision *Roe v. Wade*, which states that the right to privacy can extend to a woman's right to have an abortion.

because it violated the right to privacy in the home. The justices agreed that the Constitution does not specifically refer to a right to privacy, but that the right to privacy is suggested by the Third Amendment and several other amendments.

The right to privacy was revisited in 1972, when the Supreme Court heard the case of *Eisenstadt v. Baird*. The case involved a birth control law similar to the one in Connecticut, except it applied to unmarried couples. The court ruled to uphold the right to privacy and that all birth control matters should remain private. Both cases played a role in the landmark 1973 *Roe v. Wade* case that made abortion legal in all fifty states.

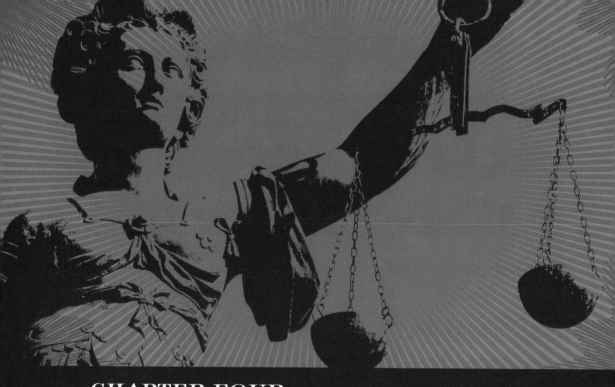

CHAPTER FOUR

THE THIRD AMENDMENT TODAY

Today, the Third Amendment is sometimes referred to as the "forgotten amendment." It has been so long since the question of quartering troops in private homes has come up that few people even consider the possibility. The United States now keeps a large standing army housed on widespread military bases connected by networks of interstate highways.

Though it isn't as frequently cited in court cases as other amendments included in the Bill of Rights, the Third Amendment continues to work as intended and with little fuss. The fact that so few court cases have ever been heard regarding the Third Amendment serves

44

Amending the Constitution

The authors of the Constitution knew that it would have to change over time if it was to endure. They wanted to make sure that changing the document would not be so easy that ill-conceived amendments could be added, but they also didn't want it to be so difficult that a change favored by most of the population would be blocked.

Amending the Constitution is a two-part process. An amendment is proposed through a two-thirds vote in each house of Congress or if two-thirds of state legislatures demand the change. After an amendment is proposed, it has to be ratified by three-fourths of the states before it becomes law. As of 2010, the Constitution had been amended twenty-seven times, including the ten amendments that make up the Bill of Rights.

as a testament to the clarity of its intentions. This may also serve as a reminder of the amendment's obscurity. During the Civil War, for example, no court challenges were made on constitutional grounds against the government for quartering soldiers. It is possible that many citizens were unaware of the amendment and the protection it provided.

The Third Amendment in Everyday Life

The Third Amendment may not be well known to many people today, but it continues to have an effect on how the government reacts to domestic emergencies. It also has had an impact on how the government houses its troops. The military has maintained forts, large military encampments, and bases throughout the nation since the Revolutionary War. During the early years of the United States, the government was

Civilian and military vehicles line up at a security checkpoint to enter Fort Dix, a military base in New Jersey. Military bases often become an important part of a region's economy and culture.

anxious to keep its soldiers out of the way of private citizens. During the eighteenth and nineteenth centuries, military forts and outposts located on the nation's frontier provided protection to civilians who faced real threats from attacking Native Americans and from the blizzards, wildfires, and other dangerous conditions that sometimes arose far from towns. When large numbers of settlers began moving west across the Great Plains, the U.S. Army established forts near major trails to protect them. Most of the vast, empty prairie was considered government land, meaning that the military did not have to worry about coming into conflict with private citizens over property rights before establishing forts.

However, soldiers often came into conflict with Native Americans. They encroached on territory that had been granted to Native American tribes and violated treaties that the tribes had signed with the federal government. While the soldiers' forts may not have been built on Native American lands, roads leading to the forts often cut through tribal territory. Sometimes, Native American leaders saw the military presence as a threat and would launch attacks against soldiers or settlers.

Settlers who ran into trouble could seek help at the nearest fort. Towns usually grew up near these forts and, in calmer parts of the country, around camps and bases. Even during the mid-twentieth century, a new military base could create a great deal of employment for a region. People would move into the area to work on the base or set up businesses that served the base workers and military personnel.

Today, many private citizens earn their living by working on or around military bases. They run businesses such as shops and restaurants that cater to soldiers, or they work on the base as civilians. Military bases continue to serve as a major source of employment for some towns and cities. When the Defense Department threatens to close military bases because of budget cuts or for other reasons, nearby residents often protest the closures. They recognize that the bases play an important role in their lives, both economically and by giving their communities a sense of identity.

Even in these towns, the line between private property and the military's jurisdiction remains sharply drawn. The Third Amendment ensures that the government provides housing on these bases for the military personnel stationed there, though some personnel may choose to live off base provided that they abide by the amendment and by civil laws. By providing these quarters for personnel as needed, the military remains ready to defend the country against attacks while ensuring that the Third Amendment is not violated.

Safeguarding Privacy and Freedom

The Third Amendment explicitly prohibits military personnel from demanding shelter in private homes during times of peace. It was written to prevent the military from exercising its power over citizens and to guarantee that it remained subordinate to civilian law, particularly within private homes. In the handful of Supreme Court rulings that have invoked the Third Amendment, it has also cast its protection against government intrusion in the home violating an unstated constitutional right to privacy. In the case *Griswold v. Connecticut*, the amendment was cited in the

Overseas military bases provide the personnel who live on them with services they need, such as this store located on a base in Kuwait.

U.S. troops move through New Orleans floodwaters in the aftermath of Hurricane Katrina. When the military responds to natural disasters, the Third Amendment protects the rights of citizens caught in the chaos.

Court's decision that some laws violated the Constitution by intruding into the private lives of citizens.

The Founding Fathers wanted to draw a distinct line between civilian life and the military while also maintaining militia forces of citizen-soldiers. Militia members did not enjoy special status when they weren't on active duty or conducting drills, and the Third Amendment protected ordinary citizens from abuses of power by militia members and regular soldiers. By drawing a sharp distinction between civilian and military life, they also wanted to protect the government from the possibility of being usurped by the military.

When it was written, the Third Amendment was ratified with very little debate and a high level of support. While there have not been any major instances of quartering for more than a century, troops have been deployed numerous times during natural disasters, such as in the aftermath of Hurricane Katrina. Without the amendment, the only protection citizens would have against military personnel coming into their homes is the self-restraint of the military itself, which could be severely stressed in the event of an emergency. Even if many Americans are unaware of the fact, this largely unremembered amendment continues to protect their rights in their own homes.

AMENDMENTS TO THE U.S. CONSTITUTION

First Amendment (proposed 1789; ratified 1791): Freedom of religion, speech, press, assembly, and petition

Second Amendment (proposed 1789; ratified 1791): Right to bear arms

Third Amendment (proposed 1789; ratified 1791): No quartering of soldiers in private houses in times of peace

Fourth Amendment (proposed 1789; ratified 1791): Interdiction of unreasonable search and seizure; requirement of search warrants

Fifth Amendment (proposed 1789; ratified 1791): Indictments; due process; self-incrimination; double jeopardy; eminent domain

Sixth Amendment (proposed 1789; ratified 1791): Right to a fair and speedy public trial; notice of accusations; confronting one's accuser; subpoenas; right to counsel

Seventh Amendment (proposed 1789; ratified 1791): Right to a trial by jury in civil cases

Eighth Amendment (proposed 1789; ratified 1791): No excessive bail and fines; no cruel or unusual punishment

Ninth Amendment (proposed 1789; ratified 1791): Protection of unenumerated rights (rights inferred from other legal rights but that are not themselves coded or enumerated in written constitution and laws)

Tenth Amendment (proposed 1789; ratified 1791): Limits the power of the federal government

Eleventh Amendment (proposed 1794; ratified 1795): Sovereign immunity (immunity of states from suits brought by out-of-state citizens and foreigners living outside of state's borders)

Twelfth Amendment (proposed 1803; ratified 1804): Revision of presidential election procedures (electoral college)

Thirteenth Amendment (proposed 1865; ratified 1865): Abolition of slavery

Fourteenth Amendment (proposed 1866; ratified 1868): Citizenship; state due process; application of Bill of Rights to states; revision to apportionment of congressional representatives; denies public office to anyone who has rebelled against the United States

Fifteenth Amendment (proposed 1869; ratified 1870): Suffrage no longer restricted by race

Sixteenth Amendment (proposed 1909; ratified 1913): Allows federal income tax

Seventeenth Amendment (proposed 1912; ratified 1913): Direct election to the U.S. Senate by popular vote

Eighteenth Amendment (proposed 1917; ratified 1919): Prohibition of alcohol

Nineteenth Amendment (proposed 1919; ratified 1920): Women's suffrage

Twentieth Amendment (proposed 1932; ratified 1933): Term commencement for Congress (January 3) and president (January 20)

Twenty-first Amendment (proposed 1933; ratified 1933): Repeal of Eighteenth Amendment (Prohibition)

Twenty-second Amendment (proposed 1947; ratified 1951): Limits president to two terms

Twenty-third Amendment (proposed 1960; ratified 1961): Representation of Washington, D.C., in electoral college

Twenty-fourth Amendment (proposed 1962; ratified 1964): Prohibition of restriction of voting rights due to nonpayment of poll taxes

Twenty-fifth Amendment (proposed 1965; ratified 1967): Presidential succession

Twenty-sixth Amendment (proposed 1971; ratified 1971): Voting age of eighteen

Twenty-seventh Amendment (proposed 1789; ratified 1992): Congressional compensation

Proposed but Unratified Amendments

Congressional Apportionment Amendment (proposed 1789; still technically pending): Apportionment of U.S. representatives

Titles of Nobility Amendment (proposed 1810; still technically pending): Prohibition of titles of nobility

Corwin Amendment (proposed 1861; still technically pending though superseded by Thirteenth Amendment): Preservation of slavery

Child Labor Amendment (proposed 1924; still technically pending): Congressional power to regulate child labor

Equal Rights Amendment (proposed 1972; expired): Prohibition of inequality of men and women

District of Columbia Voting Rights Amendment (proposed 1978; expired): District of Columbia voting rights

GLOSSARY

ambassador A high-ranking official who represents the interests of one country to another.

amendment A change or addition to a document, such as a bill or the Constitution.

assembly A body of elected political representatives, usually the lower house of a state legislature.

barracks A building or group of buildings used to house soldiers.

barter To trade goods or services without exchanging money.

bicameral A legislative body with two branches, chambers, or houses.

boycott To refuse to purchase products or services as a means of protest, or to apply pressure against an entity such as a nation, company, or organization.

colony A group of people who leave their native country to form a settlement in a new land, while maintaining ties to their home.

convention A meeting or formal gathering of representatives or delegates to discuss and act on matters of common concern.

customs Charges imposed by law on imported or exported goods.

delegate A person chosen to act for or represent others.

garrison A place where troops are stationed.

indentured servant A person who came to America and was placed under contract to work for another person over a period of time.

insurrection An act or instance of rising up in revolt, rebellion, or resistance against a civil authority or an established government.

legislature A body of officials who have been elected or chosen to make, change, or repeal laws.

militia A body of citizens signed up for military service Militia members serve full-time only in emergencies.

Parliament The legislature of Great Britain.

petition A formally composed request, often containing the names of those making the request, that has been sent to people in power to ask for some favor, right, or other benefit.

quarter To house or give lodgings.

ratify To confirm by expressing approval or consent.

regiment A unit of ground forces consisting of two or more battalions or battle groups, a headquarters unit, and supporting units.

tyrannical Unjustly cruel, harsh, or severe.

FOR MORE INFORMATION

Bill of Rights Institute
200 North Glebe Road, Suite 200
Arlington, VA 22203
(703) 894-1776
Web site: http://www.billofrightsinstitute.org
The Bill of Rights Institute's mission is to educate young people about the words and ideas of America's founders, the liberties guaranteed in America's founding documents, and the continued impact of these principles.

Bostonian Society
206 Washington Street
Boston, MA 02109
(617) 720-1713
Web site: http://www.bostonhistory.org
The Bostonian Society is dedicated to studying and preserving Boston's history in the form of historic materials, records, and structures.

Canadian War Museum
1 Vimy Place
Ottawa, ON K1A 0M8
Canada
(800) 555-5621
Web site: http://www.warmuseum.ca
The Canadian War Museum records Canadian military history from the War of 1812 to World War I.

James Madison's Montpelier

P.O. Box 911
Orange, VA 22960
(540) 672-2728
Web site: http://www.montpelier.org

Montpelier was home to James Madison and his wife, Dolly, and today houses a center for learning about Madison and his vision for a constitutional government.

National Constitution Center

Independence Mall
525 Arch Street
Philadelphia, PA 19106
(205) 409-6600
Web site: http://constitutioncenter.org

The National Constitution Center is dedicated to promoting a better understanding of and appreciation for the U.S. Constitution, its history, and its contemporary relevance.

Parliament of Canada

Information Service
Ottawa, ON K1A 0A9
Canada
(613) 992-4793
Web site: http://www.parl.gc.ca

The Canadian Parliament was established in 1867 and serves as the nation's legislative body. It is modeled after the British Parliament.

Smithsonian National Museum of American History

1000 Jefferson Drive SW
  Washington, DC 20004

(202) 633-1000

Web site: http://americanhistory.si.edu/index.cfm

The National Museum of American History has a vast collection of artifacts pertaining to American history.

U.S. National Archives and Records Administration

8601 Adelphi Road

College Park, MD 20740

(866) 272-6272

Web site: http://www.archives.gov

The National Archives and Records Administration preserves government documents and records that have historical or legal significance.

Web Sites

Due to the changing nature of Internet links, Rosen Publishing has developed an online list of Web sites related to the subject of this book. This site is updated regularly. Please use this link to access the list:

http://www.rosenlinks.com/ausc/3rd

FOR FURTHER READING

Aronson, Marc. *The Real Revolution: The Global Story of American Independence*. Boston, MA: Houghton Mifflin Harcourt, 2005.

Burgan, Michael. *The Boston Massacre*. Minneapolis, MN: Compass Point Books, 2005.

Burgan, Michael. *Soldier and Founder: Alexander Hamilton*. Minneapolis, MN: Compass Point Books, 2009.

Forbes, Esther. *Johnny Tremain*. New York, NY: Dell, 1943.

Fradin, Dennis. *The Bill of Rights*. London, UK: Marshall Cavendish, 2008.

Graham, Amy. *A Look at the Bill of Rights: Protecting the Rights of Americans*. Berkeley Heights, NJ: Enslow Publishers, 2008.

Gunderson, Megan M. *James Madison*. Edina, MN: ABDO Publishing, 2009.

Leavitt, Aime Jane. *The Bill of Rights in Translation: What It Really Means*. Mankato, MN: Capstone Press, 2008.

McGowan, Tom. *The Revolutionary War and George Washington's Army in American History*. Berkeley Heights, NJ: Enslow Publishers, 2004.

Smith, Rich. *Second and Third Amendments: The Right to Security*. Edina, MN: ABDO Publishing, 2008.

Sobel, Syl. *The Bill of Rights: Protecting Our Freedom Then and Now*. Hauppauge, NY: Barron, 2008.

Spagenburg, Ray, and Kit Moser. *Civil Liberties*. Tarrytown, NY: Marshall Cavendish Benchmark, 2006.

Thomas, William David. *What Is a Constitution?* Pleasantville, NY: Gareth Stevens, 2008.

Yero, Judith Lloyd. *The Bill of Rights*. Washington, DC: National Geographic, 2006.

BIBLIOGRAPHY

Amar, Akhil Reed. *The Bill of Rights*. New Haven, CT: Yale University Press, 1998.

Bell, Tom W. "The Third Amendment: Forgotten but not Gone." *William and Mary Bill of Rights Journal*. Williamsburg, VA: College of William and Mary, 1993. Retrieved March 8, 2010 (http://www.tomwbell.com/writings/3rd.html#HII.B.3).

Carey, Charles W., Jr., ed. *The American Revolution: Opposing Viewpoints*. Farmington Hills, MI: Greenhaven Press, 2005.

Cook, Don. *The Long Fuse: How England Lost the American Colonies, 1760–1785*. New York, NY: Atlantic Monthly Press, 1995.

Countryman, Edward. *The American Revolution*. New York, NY: Hill and Wang, 2003.

Fields, William S., and David T. Hardy. "The Third Amendment and the Issue of Standing Armies." *American Journal of Legal History*. Philadelphia, PA: Temple University, 1991. Retrieved March 8, 2010 (http://www.saf.org/LawReviews/FieldsAndHardy2.html).

Knight, Robert, and Morris MacGregor. *Soldier Statesmen of the Constitution*. Washington, DC: Center of Military History, U. S. Army, 1987.

Mitchell, Ralph. *CQ's Guide to the U.S. Constitution*. Washington, DC: Congressional Quarterly, Inc., 1994.

Monk, Linda R. *The Words We Live By: Your Annotated Guide to the Constitution*. New York, NY: Stonesong Press, 2003.

Nash, Gary B. *The Unknown American Revolution*. New York, NY: Penguin Group, 2005.

Peltrason, J. W., and Sue Davis. *Understanding the Constitution*. Orlando, FL: Harcourt College Publishers, 2000.

Rakove, Jack N. *Original Meanings: Politics and Ideas in the Making of the Constitution*. New York, NY: Vintage Books, 1996.

Roger, James P. "Third Amendment Protections in Domestic Disasters." *Cornell Journal of Law and Legal Practice*. Ithaca, NY: Cornell University Law School, 2008. Retrieved March 8, 2010 (http://www. lawschool.cornell.edu/research/JLPP/upload/Rogers.pdf).

USHistory.org. "Quartering Act of 1774." Philadelphia, PA: Independence Hall Association, 1995–2010. Retrieved March 8, 2010 (http://www.ushistory.org/Declaration/related/q74.htm).

Vile, John R. *A Companion to the United States Constitution and Its Amendments*. 4th ed. Westport, CN: Praeger Publishers, 2006.

Wright, Esmond. *Fabric of Freedom: 1763–1800*. New York, NY: Hill and Wang, 1978.

INDEX

A

American Civil War, 33, 35–38, 41, 45
American Revolution, 4, 18, 24, 26,
    28, 38, 45
Articles of Confederation, 19, 20, 21

B

Bill of Rights, 5, 23, 24–26, 33, 35,
    37, 44, 45

C

Constitutional Convention, 21–23, 24
Continental Congresses, 18–20

D

Declaration of Independence, 19, 24

E

English Bill of Rights, 13, 24

F

Federalist Papers, 23
Franklin, Benjamin, 20, 23
French and Indian War, 10–11, 28

H

Hamilton, Alexander, 23

J

Jay, John, 23
Jefferson, Thomas, 20, 24

M

Madison, James, 21, 23, 24, 28, 29,
    30, 32
Mason, George, 24

P

Posse Comitatus Act, 40–41
Proclamation Act of 1763, 12

Q

Quartering Acts, 12, 13–15, 18, 26,
    28, 29
Quebec Act, 18

S

Stamp Act, 12–13
Sugar Act of 1764, 12

T

Third Amendment
    alternate versions of, 30–32
    and civil unrest, 37–40
    creation of, 5, 26–28
    in everyday life today, 6, 47–49
    and the right to privacy, 6, 43, 49–50
    uses and abuses of, 33, 34–38, 45–47

V

Virginia Bill of Rights, 24

W

Washington, George, 20, 23, 28, 30

About the Author

Jason Porterfield is a writer and journalist living in Chicago, Illinois. He has written more than twenty books for Rosen Publishing, including *The Lincoln-Douglas Senatorial Debates of 1858: A Primary Source Investigation* and *The Treaty of Guadalupe Hidalgo, 1848: A Primary Source Examination of the Treaty That Ended the Mexican-American War.*

Photo Credits

Cover Mario Villafuerte/Getty Images; cover (inset) Keith Johnson/ Deseret Morning News/Getty Images; p. 1 (top) www.istockphoto.com/ Tom Nulens; p. 1 (bottom) www.istockphoto.com/Lee Pettet; p. 3 www. istockphoto.com/Nic Taylor; pp. 4–5 U.S. Air Force; pp. 7, 20, 33, 44 © www.istockphoto.com/arturbo; pp. 8–9 Henry Guttmann/Getty Images; pp. 10–11, 16, 25, 36 MPI/Getty Images; pp. 14, 31, 38–39 Library of Congress Prints and Photographs Division; p. 22 Stock Montage/Stock Montage/Getty Images; p. 27 Hulton Archive/Getty Images; p. 34 Master Sgt. Jim Varhegyi/U.S. Air Force; p. 42 Lee Lockwood/Time & Life Pictures/Getty Images; p. 46 Bradley C. Bower/Bloomberg/Getty Images; pp. 48–49 Journalist 1st Class Joseph Krypel/U.S. Navy; p. 50 U.S. Air Force.

Photo Researcher: Amy Feinberg